Francis Frith's
Taunton

Photographic Memories

Francis Frith's
Taunton

John Bainbridge

First published in the United Kingdom in 2001 by
Frith Book Company Ltd

Paperback Edition 2001
ISBN 1-85937-314-3

British Library Cataloguing in Publication Data

Francis Frith's Taunton
John Bainbridge

Frith Book Company Ltd
Frith's Barn, Teffont,
Salisbury, Wiltshire SP3 5QP
Tel: +44 (0) 1722 716 376
Email: info@francisfrith.co.uk
www.francisfrith.co.uk

Printed and bound in Great Britain

Front Cover: North Street 1906 56782

Contents

Francis Frith: *Victorian Pioneer*

FRANCIS FRITH, Victorian founder of the world-famous photographic archive, was a complex and multi-talented man. A devout Quaker and a highly successful Victorian businessman, he was both philosophic by nature and pioneering in outlook.

By 1855 Francis Frith had already established a wholesale grocery business in Liverpool, and sold it for the astonishing sum of £200,000, which is the equivalent today of over £15,000,000. Now a multi-millionaire, he was able to indulge his passion for travel. As a child he had pored over travel books written by early explorers, and his fancy and imagination had been stirred by family holidays to the sublime mountain regions of Wales and Scotland. 'What a land of spirit-stirring and enriching scenes and places!' he had written. He was to return to these scenes of grandeur in later years to 'recapture the thousands of vivid and tender memories', but with a different purpose. Now in his thirties, and captivated by the new science of photography, Frith set out on a series of pioneering journeys to the Nile regions that occupied him from 1856 until 1860.

Intrigue and Adventure

He took with him on his travels a specially-designed wicker carriage that acted as both dark-room and sleeping chamber. These far-flung journeys were packed with intrigue and adventure. In his life story, written when he was sixty-three, Frith tells of being held captive by bandits, and of fighting 'an awful midnight battle to the very point of surrender with a deadly pack of hungry, wild dogs'. Sporting flowing Arab costume, Frith arrived at Akaba by camel seventy years before Lawrence, where he encountered 'desert princes and rival sheikhs, blazing with jewel-hilted swords'.

During these extraordinary adventures he was assiduously exploring the desert regions bordering the Nile and patiently recording the antiquities and peoples with his camera. He was the first photographer to venture beyond the sixth cataract. Africa was still the mysterious 'Dark Continent', and Stanley and Livingstone's historic meeting was a decade into the future. The conditions for picture taking confound belief. He laboured for hours in his wicker dark-room in the sweltering heat of the desert, while the volatile chemicals fizzed dangerously in their trays. Often he was forced to work in remote tombs and caves where conditions were cooler. Back in London he exhibited his photographs and was 'rapturously cheered' by members of the Royal Society. His reputation as a

photographer was made overnight. An eminent modern historian has likened their impact on the population of the time to that on our own generation of the first photographs taken on the surface of the moon.

Venture of a Life-Time

Characteristically, Frith quickly spotted the opportunity to create a new business as a specialist publisher of photographs. He lived in an era of immense and sometimes violent change. For the poor in the early part of Victoria's reign work was a drudge and the hours long, and people had precious little free time to enjoy themselves. Most had no transport other than a cart or gig at their disposal, and had not travelled far beyond the boundaries of their own town or village. However,

by the 1870s, the railways had threaded their way across the country, and Bank Holidays and half-day Saturdays had been made obligatory by Act of Parliament. All of a sudden the ordinary working man and his family were able to enjoy days out and see a little more of the world.

With characteristic business acumen, Francis Frith foresaw that these new tourists would enjoy having souvenirs to commemorate their days out. In 1860 he married Mary Ann Rosling and set out with the intention of photographing every city, town and village in Britain. For the next thirty years he travelled the country by train and by pony and trap, producing fine photographs of seaside resorts and beauty spots that were keenly bought by millions of Victorians. These prints were painstakingly pasted into family albums and pored over during the dark nights of winter, rekindling precious memories of summer excursions.

The Rise of Frith & Co

Frith's studio was soon supplying retail shops all over the country. To meet the demand he gathered about him a small team of photographers, and published the work of independent artist-photographers of the calibre of Roger Fenton and Francis Bedford. In order to gain some understanding of the scale of Frith's business one only has to look at the catalogue issued by Frith & Co in 1886: it runs to some 670 pages, listing not only many thousands of views of the British Isles but also many photographs of most European countries, and China, Japan, the USA and Canada – note the sample page shown above from the hand-written *Frith & Co* ledgers detailing pictures taken. By 1890 Frith had created the greatest specialist photographic publishing company in the world,

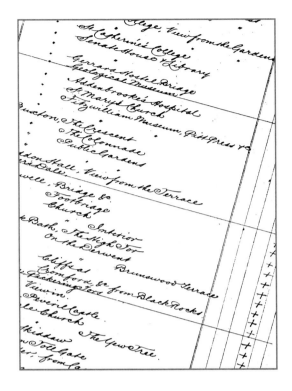

Frith's death, a new card measuring 5.5 x 3.5 inches became the standard format, but it was not until 1902 that the divided back came into being, with address and message on one face and a full-size illustration on the other. *Frith & Co* were in the vanguard of postcard development, and Frith's sons Eustace and Cyril continued their father's monumental task, expanding the number of views offered to the public and recording more and more places in Britain, as the coasts and countryside were opened up to mass travel.

Francis Frith died in 1898 at his villa in Cannes, his great project still growing. The archive he created continued in business for another seventy years. By 1970 it contained over a third of a million pictures of 7,000 cities, towns and villages. The massive photographic record Frith has left to us stands as a living monument to a special and very remarkable man.

with over 2,000 outlets – more than the combined number that Boots and W H Smith have today! The picture on the right shows the *Frith & Co* display board at Ingleton in the Yorkshire Dales. Beautifully constructed with mahogany frame and gilt inserts, it could display up to a dozen local scenes.

Postcard Bonanza

The ever-popular holiday postcard we know today took many years to develop. In 1870 the Post Office issued the first plain cards, with a pre-printed stamp on one face. In 1894 they allowed other publishers' cards to be sent through the mail with an attached adhesive halfpenny stamp. Demand grew rapidly, and in 1895 a new size of postcard was permitted called the court card, but there was little room for illustration. In 1899, a year after

Frith's Archive: *A Unique Legacy*

FRANCIS FRITH'S legacy to us today is of immense significance and value, for the magnificent archive of evocative photographs he created provides a unique record of change in 7,000 cities, towns and villages throughout Britain over a century and more. Frith and his fellow studio photographers revisited locations many times down the years to update their views, compiling for us an enthralling and colourful pageant of British life and character.

We tend to think of Frith's sepia views of Britain as nostalgic, for most of us use them to conjure up memories of places in our own lives with which we have family associations. It often makes us forget that to Francis Frith they were records of daily life as it was actually being lived in the cities, towns and villages of his day. The Victorian age was one of great and often bewildering change for ordinary people, and though the pictures evoke an impression of slower times, life was as busy and hectic as it is today.

We are fortunate that Frith was a photographer of the people, dedicated to recording the minutiae of everyday life. For it is this sheer wealth of visual data, the painstaking chronicle of changes in dress, transport, street layouts, buildings, housing, engineering and landscape that captivates us so much today. His remarkable images offer us a powerful link with the past and with the lives of our ancestors.

Today's Technology

Computers have now made it possible for Frith's many thousands of images to be accessed almost instantly. In the Frith archive today, each photograph is carefully 'digitised' then stored on a CD Rom. Frith archivists can locate a single photograph amongst thousands within seconds. Views can be catalogued and sorted under a variety of categories of place and content to the immediate benefit of researchers.

Inexpensive reference prints can be created for them at the touch of a mouse button, and a wide range of books and other printed materials assembled and published for a wider, more general readership - in the next twelve months over a hundred Frith local history titles will be published! The day-to-day workings of the archive are very different from how they were in Francis Frith's time: imagine the herculean task of sorting through eleven tons of glass negatives as Frith had to do to locate a particular sequence of pictures! Yet

THE FRANCIS FRITH COLLECTION
Photographic publishers since 1860

HOME | PHOTO SEARCH | BOOKS | PORTFOLIO | GALLERY   MY CART
Products | History | Other Collections | Contact us | Help?

your town,
your village

365,000
photographs of 7,000 towns and villages, taken between 1860 & 1970.

The Frith Archive
The Frith Archive is the remarkable legacy of its energetic and visionary founder. Today, the Frith archive is the only nationally important archive of its kind still in private ownership.

The Collection is world-renowned for the extraordinary quality of its images.

The Gallery
This month The Frith Gallery features images from "Frith's Egypt".

the FRITHgallery

News...
Image update complete.
An additional 5,000 images have been added and the quality of all images has now been improved.

Sample Chapters available.
The first selection of sample chapters from the Frith Book Co.'s extensive range is now available. All are offered in Pdf format for easy downloading and viewing.

explore
FRITH
Search thousands of photographs from one of the worlds' great archives.

Town search

County search
Select a county

See Frith at www.francisfrith.co.uk

the archive still prides itself on maintaining the same high standards of excellence laid down by Francis Frith, including the painstaking cataloguing and indexing of every view.

It is curious to reflect on how the internet now allows researchers in America and elsewhere greater instant access to the archive than Frith himself ever enjoyed. Many thousands of individual views can be called up on screen within seconds on one of the Frith internet sites, enabling people living continents away to revisit the streets of their ancestral home town, or view places in Britain where they have enjoyed holidays. Many overseas researchers welcome the chance to view special theme selections, such as transport, sports, costume and ancient monuments.

We are certain that Francis Frith would have heartily approved of these modern developments in imaging techniques, for he himself was always working at the very limits of Victorian photographic technology.

The Value of the Archive Today

Because of the benefits brought by the computer, Frith's images are increasingly studied by social historians, by researchers into genealogy and ancestory, by architects, town planners, and by teachers and schoolchildren involved in local history projects.

In addition, the archive offers every one of us an opportunity to examine the places where we and our families have lived and worked down the years. Highly successful in Frith's own era, the archive is now, a century and more on, entering a new phase of popularity.

The Past in Tune with the Future

Historians consider the Francis Frith Collection to be of prime national importance. It is the only archive of its kind remaining in private ownership and has been valued at a million pounds. However, this figure is now rapidly increasing as digital technology enables more and more people around the world to enjoy its benefits.

Francis Frith's archive is now housed in an historic timber barn in the beautiful village of Teffont in Wiltshire. Its founder would not recognize the archive office as it is today. In place of the many thousands of dusty boxes containing glass plate negatives and an all-pervading odour of photographic chemicals, there are now ranks of computer screens. He would be amazed to watch his images travelling round the world at unimaginable speeds through network and internet lines.

The archive's future is both bright and exciting. Francis Frith, with his unshakeable belief in making photographs available to the greatest number of people, would undoubtedly approve of what is being done today with his lifetime's work. His photographs, depicting our shared past, are now bringing pleasure and enlightenment to millions around the world a century and more after his death.

Taunton - *An Introduction*

Many an English town has had brushes with England's history, but few can boast such an interesting record of conflict and rebellion as Taunton. Many an important historical figure has passed this way, leaving a mark upon both local and national history, from Saxon warlords to Norman conquerors, from ecclesiastical scholars to Tudor kings, from rebels to cloth-weavers.

There is little evidence of much of a settlement on the site of present day Taunton before the Saxon King Ine drove the Britons out of the lush pastures along the River Tone in the year 688. The evidence of Ine's foundation is slender but likely, for the 'Anglo-Saxon Chronicle' relates that in 722 Queen Aethelburg 'destroyed Taunton, which King Ine had formerly built'. These rich agricultural lands which we now know as Taunton Deane were worth fighting over, for the Saxons were competent and ambitious farmers as well as doughty warriors.

The Taunton of Ine's day was a collection of small thatched huts, grouped around an earthwork enclosure of which some slender evidence remains. It is likely that it was Ine, a deeply religious man, who gave the Saxon manor of Taunton to the See of Winchester - a connection that endured for several centuries. In later Saxon times a minster stood

close to the site of Ine's fortification, though nothing of it survives. Conflicts with the Danes brought Alfred to the area, organising guerrilla operations deep in the marshlands of nearby Athelney. Marauding Vikings burnt the town in 1001, though it was quickly rebuilt. The settlement had increased in size by the time of the Norman Conquest sixty-five years later.

Many people imagine that William the Conqueror's invasion started and finished at Hastings in 1066, but this was not so. The West held out for a few years, and was subjected to a bloody domination by the Norman forces. However, the Domesday Book in 1086 gives an impression of a very busy agricultural community, by then firmly under the Norman yoke. These statistics are quite interesting: 265 labourers worked the land belonging to the Bishop of Winchester, using some 60 ploughs between them. 70 of these were bondmen, effectively indentured slaves. A further 64 burgesses or freemen lived in the growing town. In addition there were 3 mills worth 95 shillings a year and a market, which made an annual profit of 50 shillings. The town mint produced coinage to the profit of 50 shillings. A quick analysis of these figures, estimating the appropriate number of women and children, suggests a mostly Saxon population of around 1,600, dominated by a Norman militia and bureaucracy.

Parts of the Castle, seen in the photographs that follow, date back to late Norman times, when Henry de Blois, brother of King Stephen, fortified the town during that dark period of internecine conflict known as the Anarchy.

Taunton next features in English history when the impostor Perkin Warbeck, posing as a son of Edward IV, rode into town having failed to capture Exeter. It is unclear just what reception he received from the townsfolk. Probably bemused indifference, for he marched quickly away again on a September midnight in 1497. Recaptured, he was brought back to Taunton to confess his impudence to a wrathful Henry VII. The king apparently held no grudge against the townsfolk, for not only did he accept lavish hospitality at the Priory, but he probably contributed to the cost of building the original tower at St Mary Magdalene's Church.

The conflicts of the English Civil War affected Taunton greatly. In 1645, the Parliamentarian Admiral Robert Blake defended the town against a prolonged Royalist siege, declaring that he would eat his boots before he surrendered. The relieving forces of Sir Thomas Fairfax spared Blake this indignity - and the town from almost absolute destruction, the resistance and victory helping the defeat of the King's army in the west. There was to be little retribution for this act of *lese majeste* from Charles II on his restoration, though the town's charter was suspended for a while.

Taunton was not so lucky forty years on, during the Duke of Monmouth's ill-fated rebellion. Monmouth, the illegitimate son of Charles II, was

proclaimed king in the town and given a rapturous welcome by the townsfolk, a number of whom joined his sickle and scythe army on its way to final defeat out on the marshes of Sedgemoor. Retribution for this treason was to be swift and merciless. After the battle, Colonel Kirke's victorious regiment, his 'lambs' as they were nicknamed, fresh from foreign slaughter in Tangier, brought prisoners back to the town, hanging 30 in the market place, even as Kirke enjoyed a supper at the White Hart tavern. Three months later the infamous Judge Jeffreys presided over a Bloody Assize in the Great Hall of the Castle. Taunton folk were amongst those sentenced to death or transportation. The town had played a heavy price for its flirtation with treason.

But history is not just made by kings, judges and bishops. The social history of ordinary folk is every bit as important, and no more so than in a town such as Taunton, where their efforts led to growth and economic development. The two traditional industries of Taunton Deane were cloth production and agriculture. In a sense one was dependent upon the other, for wool provided the raw material for the cloth, not least the rough serge known as 'Taunton Cloth'. Flemish weavers had settled in the locality in the 14th century, bringing new techniques to what had been a simple home-based craft in earlier times. Merchant families became prominent, and participated in the affairs and expansion of the town. Agriculturally, Taunton Deane has always been a productive and prosperous region, as it is today. It was the riches from both of these trades that led to the construction of Taunton's finest buildings, not least its churches with their soaring towers.

This is not to say that everything was peaceful. Times were hard in the last two centuries; Taunton suffered its share of riots and social protests, as working people sought a share in the wealth generated by their industry. Reaction to these disputes was often harsh. In 1801 nine local men were hanged at Stone Gallows on the Wellington road, their only crime stealing bread for their hungry families.

In mid-Victorian times, old Taunton town began to change from its old medieval layout to much the street pattern we see today - the one which is depicted in these photographs. This was the great age of civic reconstruction. Old churches were restored, in Taunton's case quite sympathetically, and new municipal buildings rose as fast as old insanitary slums were demolished. Whole new roads were laid out, such as the aptly-named Corporation Street, and shops were founded. Railways brought new residents and visitors to Taunton, and modern industries were founded on the edge of the town.

It is still possible to walk around present-day Taunton to see the streets pictured in this book, and often to stand in the very footsteps of the people featured within. It is, in fact, somewhat safer, for both High Street and Fore Street have been

pedestrianised, so the explorer is able to linger and compare scenes in comfort. Many of the buildings shown in this book survive, though there has been a bewildering change in the design of shop fronts.

The way traffic is controlled as the 20th century progresses is shown in detail in the following pages. We see the first attempts at traffic islands, the phasing out of horse-drawn conveyances and trams, and early parking arrangements. The pictures of the Parade, in particular, give some idea of just how ruthless municipal planners could be where allowance for the motor car had to be made. They did not hesitate to destroy or relocate monuments and trees, turn paved areas into roadways, or send cars across places where people had formerly sat and relaxed.

As important as the buildings and streets are the people illustrated in these photographs. They are as much a part of Taunton's history as King Ine, Monmouth or Jeffreys. For history is made by such participants in the general scene. See how they are dressed, how many wear hats, and how they might regard the Frith photographer. These are real people with their own histories, hopes and worries, going about the daily task.

And as you walk around Taunton, watch out for the photographer taking your picture. Perhaps a hundred years hence someone will be turning the pages of a book similar to this one, wondering just who you were. For the long history of Taunton goes on.

Old Taunton Town

From the Bridge 1897 40802
Taunton lies at the very heart of Somerset, with the Quantock and
Brendon Hills and Exmoor to the west and the low-lying marshes of
the Somerset levels to the east. This ancient borough takes its
name from the River Tone, which winds through the town.

Roughmoor 1888 20874A
Taunton is the county town of Somerset and has thrived from its setting on the fertile plain of Taunton Deane. Even the decline of the wool trade had little effect on the town, for agriculture helped stave off the hard times. The poet Michael Drayton asked 'What ear so empty is, they hath not heard the sound of Taunton's fruitful Deane?'

Church Tower View 1929 82089
A splendid view over the heart of Taunton town. In late Victorian times many of the old buildings of Taunton were demolished and new streets were created. Notice the early marked parking spaces in the street below.

Priory Lock 1888 20873
The Priory Fields are a reminder of the Augustinian priory, which once stood nearby. Priory Barn, once the gatehouse, serves as the Somerset Cricket Museum.

French Weir 1906 55800

French Weir 1906 55801
Taunton is a town surrounded by water, with the Tone passing through its heart and the marshes not far away. It is still possible to walk along the banks of the local waterways, just as these Edwardian children did nearly a century ago. A canal to Tiverton once started from French Weir.

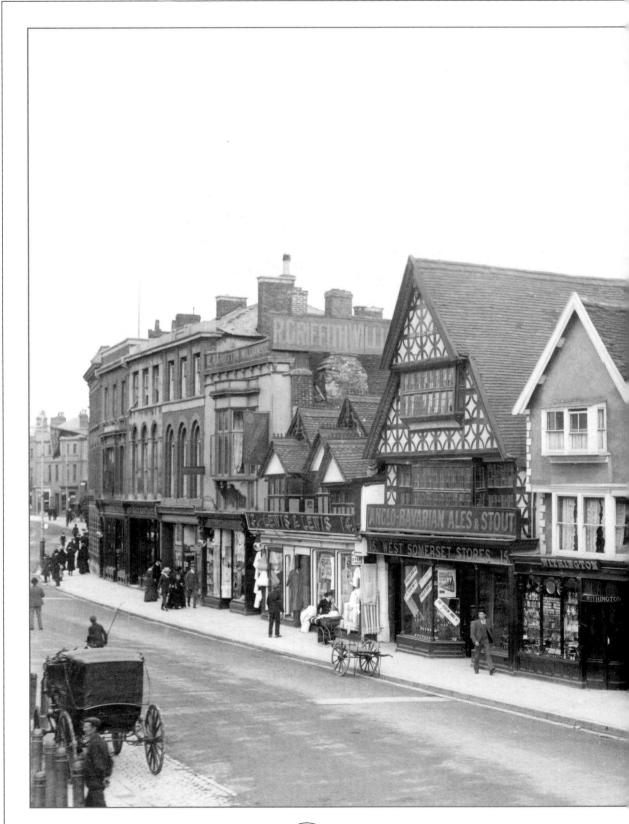

Fore Street 1902
48723
Where better to begin an exploration of Taunton town than in Fore Street, very much the centre of this ancient Borough. The Devon and Somerset Stores, seen here amongst many excellent shop fronts, has posters in the window advertising Frister Russman Sewing Machines at £3 7s 6d and £2 18s 6d.

Fore Street 1902

48720

This scene has changed considerably since this photograph was taken at the junction of Fore Street and East Street. The memorial cross has been relocated to the Parade, the trams are no more and Fore Street has been pedestrianised. The carriage on the left is the private conveyance of the London Hotel, just around the corner.

Fore Street 1906 56778
The cross, usually called the Burmese War Memorial, has marked upon it the battle honours of the Somerset Regiment, including Jellalabad 1841-42, the Crimea 1854, Burma 1885 and South Africa 1899-1902. A 20th-century war memorial stands some distance away in Vivary Park.

Fore Street 1906 56777
The double-decker trams eventually gave way to single-deckers, as seen here. On the left-hand side of the street is F W Baker's music shop. The notice at the top of the building offers 'Pianos and Organs on the 3 Years System' - a form of hire purchase.

Fore Street 1912 64507
The Tudor House in Fore Street is even older than its name suggests, for it dates to the 14th century and is the most ancient building in the town. The present Elizabethan frontage dates back to 1578.

**Fore Street
Old Houses 1912**
64506
Several of these lovely old buildings remain, though the shop fronts have changed. This part of Fore Street is now a pedestrian precinct with trees, flower beds and benches lining the side of the road where the Frith photographer would have stood to take this picture.

Fore Street 1925
78807
The Tudor House has
most recently seen
service as a public
house. In the heyday of
Taunton market there
were some twenty inns
in this area of the town.

▼ **Fore Street, Looking East 1935** 86820
Even in the 1930s, Taunton was starting to experience traffic problems; hence the bewildering change in roundabouts and other control measures through this sequence of photographs. This particular roundabout didn't last very long.

▼ **Fore Street c1950** T16030
The Market House, seen here on the left, was built in 1772 and has fulfilled a variety of roles since. In this photograph we see it as a branch office of the Alliance Assurance Company - notice the Alliance sign on the right-hand edge of the wall. Today it houses the offices of Age Concern and a school of dance.

▲ **Cheapside c1950**
T16027
A great deal of older residential housing was demolished in Victorian times to make way for Cheapside. There are now new shopping centres in the vicinity of this commercial area of the town.

◀ **The County Hotel 1925**
78814
A motorcyclist loads his sidecar outside the County Hotel, renamed from the London Hotel. On the left-hand side of the road are the Army and Navy Stores and a shop selling stuffed birds.

East Street 1902
48724
A very busy street seen here in the second year of Edward VII's reign. It is still possible to see much the same scene today, though the transport and fashion has changed. The buildings to the left have survived, though all have acquired a change of use. The London Hotel, now a bookshop, owned the stagecoach rights to the Capital. The horse-bus in front of the portico was used to convey guests to and from the railway station.

East Street 1929
82091
The hotel began its life
in Tudor times as the
Three Cups Tavern,
before becoming the
London Hotel and then
the County Hotel. The
alley to the right of the
hotel building now leads
to the New Market
Shopping Centre.

◄ **East Street c1950**
T16028
A stroll along present day East Street from the town centre to East Reach is a fascinating experience for any would-be town historian. Despite some unimaginative modern intrusions, a number of these old Georgian and Victorian buildings may be identified above the present day shop fronts.

East Street 1938 88473
East Street is still one of Taunton's busiest streets and remains a thoroughfare for motor traffic. It was once part of the main highway from London to Exeter, and many a mail and stagecoach passed this way. The Victorian Phoenix Hotel is a replacement for the very ancient inn of the same name, which once stood on the site.

East Reach 1902 48743
East Street leads into East Reach beyond which, until the last century, was open countryside. The two streets were once separated by East Gate, the old boundary of Taunton Borough. The gate was built in 910 and destroyed during the Civil War. Nearby is a charming row of almshouses.

High Street 1925
78808
A wonderful collection of old motor cars in Taunton's High Street. This once busy highway is now pedestrianised; a place to sit or saunter amongst trees, benches and pavement cafes.

▼ High Street c1950 T16013

It was at the northern end of High Street that the unfortunate Duke of Monmouth was declared king in 1685. After the failure of his rebellion at the Battle of Sedgemoor, a number of his local followers were executed at the same spot.

▼ The Park Gates 1906 55797

Crossing Mary Street from the southern end of the High Street brings the explorer of Taunton to Vivary Park. Two fishponds - or vivaria - belonging to the Bishops of Winchester were to be found here in the Middle Ages. These impressive gates, restored in 2001, bear the legend Borough of Taunton and the motto Defendamus.

▲ The Park
The Fountain 1902
64510

This impressive fountain commemorates Queen Victoria's Diamond Jubilee. Vivary Park was purchased in 1894 and a bandstand and the gates were added the following year. The park has been recently renovated with the help of a National Lottery grant.

◄ **The War Memorial, Vivary Park 1935** 86826
Taunton has always had strong links with the military. This war memorial was built just after the Great War, to commemorate the fallen.

◀ **The Public Library
1906** 55794
Across the road from
the Municipal Buildings
is the old public library.
This building is now a
busy public house, for a
new state-of-the-art
library stands not far
away.

The Municipal Buildings
1902 48727

If we turn left from the High Street and into Corporation Street, the Municipal Buildings come into view. Corporation Street itself is one of the town's newer highways, dating only to 1894. The right-hand end of these buildings dates to 1522, and was originally the town grammar school. The property was purchased by the Borough in 1897 for municipal use and was extended five years later. The Municipal Buildings now act as the mayor's parlour and the local council chamber.

Corporation Street
1935 86825

Purpose-built cinemas attracted huge audiences during the great days of film going in the 1930s. When this photograph was taken, a double feature was on offer: 'Behold My Wife' and 'Death at Broadcasting House' - the latter based on the play written by Val Gielgud, brother of the famous actor.

The Castle Hotel
c1869 4937

Taunton was fortified from an early date. The earthwork of the Saxon King Ine's fort stood not far from the remnants of the later medieval castle. Ine made Taunton his headquarters after his defeat of the Welsh, using it as a base to defend the embryonic kingdom of Wessex.

The Castle 1894 34884
The castle was extended by the powerful bishops of Winchester and used by the Normans to subdue the heart of the former Saxon kingdom. An early constable was Thomas Chaucer, the son of the author of 'The Canterbury Tales'.

Clarke's Hotel 1902 48732
Clarke's is now the Castle Hotel, and two storeys higher than the building pictured here. Famous guests have included a Russian Tsar, the Emperor of Mexico, British royalty and the Duke of Wellington.

The Castle Courtyard 1906 55795
Cromwellian Admiral Robert Blake held the castle for Parliament during the Civil War, holding the town until relieved by the army of General Fairfax. At the Restoration Charles II, annoyed at the resistance, suspended the town's charter for several years.

The Castle, Jury and Witness Room 1906 55796
After the Duke of Monmouth's failed rebellion, the victorious Colonel Kirke summarily hanged over thirty rebels in Taunton's market place. More local people were condemned to death or transportation after Judge Jeffreys' Bloody Assize in the town.

Castle Square c1940 T16017
A glimpse through the Castle Bow towards the Castle Green. This area was once the site of the Saxon Minster and burial ground. In recent centuries the green was used for livestock markets.

St Mary Magdalene's Church and Hammet Street 1888 20858
Sir Benjamin Hammet, Member of Parliament, created Hammet Street in 1790. The thoroughfare opened up this impressive view of St Mary Magdalene's church. The street was an important residential area in Victorian times, and now houses a number of lawyers' offices.

St Mary Magdalene's Church 1888 20859
This 163ft church tower, built of Old Red Quantock Sandstone and Ham Hill Stone, dominates the skyline of Taunton. It is one of the most beautiful of many exquisite church towers in Somerset, despite being a reconstruction. The tower was rebuilt in 1862 to the lines of the original 15th-century design.

St Mary Magdalene's Church 1888 20862
It was Sir John Betjeman, Poet Laureate, who said that 'no county comes up to Somerset' as far as churches go.
A religious building has stood on this site since at least the 12th century. During the 1862 rebuilding, a donkey
powered the pulley which took the stone to the top of the tower. At the tower's completion the donkey was taken
up the church tower to admire the view!

Market Place 1886
19074
An Act of Parliament in 1817 allowed the enlargement of Taunton's market place. During the days of prizefighting many a bout was held in this great open space, with spectators coming from all over England. When the authorities frowned on such activities, prizefighting relocated to more discreet locations in the neighbouring countryside.

▼ **The Parade c1869** 4943
The Parade, seen here with North Street in the distance, is at the very heart of Taunton. On the left are the Victoria Rooms, built as a market in 1821 and sadly demolished in 1963.

▼ **Market Place 1902** 48742
Taunton was not always the peaceful town we know today. Industrial disputes and rural rebellions brought conflicts and riots to its streets. On one occasion the spinners and weavers of Taunton raided the town gaol to liberate compatriots who had been locked away after earlier disturbances.

▲ **The Parade, Kinglake Monument 1912** 64499
Alexander William Kinglake, the author of 'Eothen', served with Lord Raglan in the Crimean War and wrote many books about his travels. Kinglake loved Taunton, and once imagined he could hear its church bells when far away in Egypt. This monument was demolished some seventy years ago, much to the anger of the townsfolk.

◀ **The Parade 1923** 74033
The presence of so many merchants in Taunton probably explains the independent line taken by local folk in political matters - not always in their best interests. In 1497 the impostor Perkin Warbeck was proclaimed king in the town. During the Civil War the Borough supported Parliament. In 1685 Monmouth was declared king in its High Street. Taunton suffered much retribution for such rebellious activities.

The Market 1925 78812
A busy market day in the first decade of peace after the Great War. This was probably the last period in Taunton's history before motor cars became a serious problem. Today the Parade is a busy traffic junction. The smaller of the buildings to the right of the Victoria Rooms had been adapted into a cinema known simply as The Picture House when this photograph was taken.

The Parade and North Street 1929 82090
The Parade has been a place of celebration as well as dispute throughout Taunton's history. After the welcome passing of the Reform Bill in the 19th century, all the tradesmen of the town processed through the streets before enjoying a sumptuous feast here.

The Parade 1935 86818

The Parade and Market House 1935 86819
By the 1930s we see a Parade that is not so different from the one we know today. The Kinglake Monument has gone, and the streets around have created a traffic junction here, with obvious parking restrictions. Greater changes were still to come.

North Street 1902
48721
A stroll from Fore Street and the much-changed Parade brings the explorer of old Taunton to North Street. This is one of the town's most important highways, leading down to an ancient crossing point over the River Tone.

▼ **The Parade c1950** T16020

Fifty years on from this photograph, the benches and gardens have vanished and the Parade has been transformed into one of Taunton's busiest roundabouts. The Burmese War Memorial has been relocated to here, though rather incongruously on an often-inaccessible traffic island. It is interesting to imagine just what the Parade will look like in a further fifty years.

▼ **North Street 1906** 56782

The Castle Hotel, seen here on the left with the porticoed entrance, began life as the Castle Tap, a much humbler tavern, popular with stagecoach folk, postboys and market traders. The Victorian commentator Edward Goldsworthy tells us that in his youth the landlord was one Jim Saunders, 'who went to the tap so often that at last Death tapped upon his shoulder'.

▲ **North Street 1925**
78809
Few policemen would saunter across busy North Street today, as this bobby can in 1925. Notice the street light strung above the carriageway. Some of Taunton's streets were lit by electricity as early as 1886. In the distance, on the side of a building, is the advertising sign for W & A Chapman, house furnishers and undertakers.

◀ **North Street 1925** 78811
Looking back up North Street towards the Parade and Market House, with the Post Office on the left, as it still is today. It is interesting to observe how many people wore hats or caps in the first half of the last century. Apart from the occasional sun hat on a hot day, such headwear is unusual in North Street today.

◀ **The Town Bridge 1902**
48734
A splendid view of the bridge over the River Tone, with some excellent examples of advertising hoardings in the background. A Singer sewing machine shop is to be seen on the right, above the river. The advertisement for the Somerset County Gazette boasts that it is the 'only series printed in Taunton'.

North Street c1945
T16010
A couple of decades on, and the streets of Taunton are starting to become cluttered with parked motor vehicles. It has to be remembered that the large car parks so familiar to us today are a relatively recent innovation. Chapman's Department Store can be seen here, on the same site as in photograph 78811.

Bridge Street 1923 74034
There was probably some sort of crossing point over the Tone near to here in Saxon times, though the first recorded mention of a bridge was in 1280. By all accounts, Taunton's medieval bridge was an impressive six-span arched structure, though only 9' 10" at its narrowest point. The present bridge dates only to 1896; it was strengthened in 1935, and repaired and renovated at the beginning of the present century.

Elm Grove 1901 48740
Hundreds of houses in old Taunton were torn down during Victorian times and throughout the 20th century, particularly in the aftermath of the First World War. Many Taunton families and thousands of incomers were relocated on to the vast new housing estates that sprang up around and beyond the borough boundary.

Honiton Road 1902 48738
In earlier times, the surroundings of Taunton were as peaceful as this scene suggests. It is still possible to find such quiet corners in and around the town, though the motorway, approach roads and industrial development have eaten up many of the green fields of the Deane.

Park Street 1906 55792
Most of the Park Street houses seen here are Victorian, for this was one of the original suburbs of the old town, built at a time when rural England was being transformed into urban and industrial England. The church at the end of Park Street is St John's.

The Independent College 1888 20869
Taunton School was founded as the Independent College in the 1840s and located in a street in the heart of town. These buildings date from the 1870s when the college relocated in search of more space to expand. Independent College was renamed as Taunton School in 1899.

Queen's College 1894 34881
Queen's College began to educate the young within the walls of Taunton Castle, before moving out to the open countryside close to the village of Trull. It is a quite splendid example of Victorian architecture.

▼ **King's College 1902** 48719
King's College is the oldest educational foundation in Taunton, for it dates to medieval times when it enjoyed the patronage of the Bishops of Winchester. The growth of the school led to its expansion in Victorian times, hence these buildings. In olden days horse races were held on this site.

▼ **The Taunton and Somerset Hospital 1902** 48741
Taunton celebrated King George III's Jubilee by building a new hospital for the town. It opened for patients in March 1812, with four wards and 26 beds. It was enlarged on several occasions throughout Victorian times. A modern hospital at Musgrove Park now serves the needs of the people of Taunton.

▲ **The Shire Hall c1869**
4964
The Shire Hall was built as a gesture towards municipal pride at the height of Victoria's reign. It stands on the former site of a large house called The Grove, once the home of Colonel Pearson, a local worthy.

◀ The Shire Hall 1894

34879

Taunton had neither a Mayor nor a Corporation for much of the 19th century: its affairs were administered by the Market Trust. However, a new charter was granted in 1877, and a Mayor and Corporation were appointed. The Market Trust struggled on, but it was finally abolished in 1926.

The Barracks 1894

34893

Taunton has had a long connection with the military: a cavalry barracks was built as long ago as 1796. The Somerset Regiment saw action during the Napoleonic Wars and in most of the conflicts of the next two centuries.

**◄ St James's Church
1912** 64516
A Norman church once
stood on this site. The
present building dates to
the 15th century,
although there has been
a great deal of Victorian
restoration. The
medieval font and the
Jacobean pulpit are
outstanding, making this
church well worth a visit.

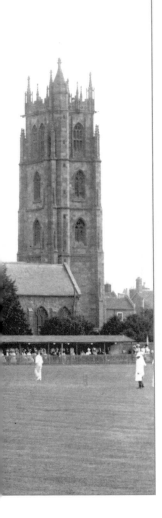

◀ **The County Cricket Ground 1902** 48716
A cricket match on the County Ground is still a familiar site during a summer in Taunton, as it has been since the club was founded in 1875. Apart from some minor changes to the pavilion and the removal of the factory chimney, little has changed.

▼ **St Andrew's Church 1912** 64513
St Andrew's, with its attractive spire, is one of the newer places of worship in Taunton, being completed in 1881. The rapid growth of the town in Victorian times led to the creation of a new parish - much of the ground was taken in from the older parish of St James. Notice the tramlines and cables on and above the road.

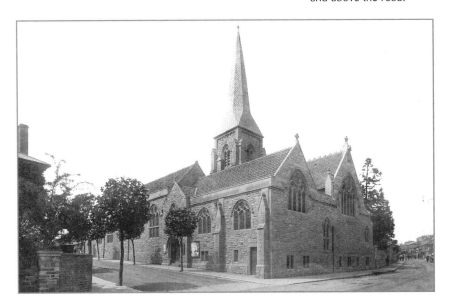

◀ **County Hall 1938**
88471
Despite the importance of nearby cities such as Bath or the cathedral city of Wells, Taunton proudly remains the County Town of Somerset. This new County Hall was built on the outskirts of old Taunton town in the 1930s.

Around and About

Taunton is blessed with a delightful setting in the heart of Somerset. Even with the construction of the M5 motorway and new housing and industrial estates, it remains very much a country town, with people from the neighbouring villages making a weekly visit to shop.

At the time when these photographs were taken, the villages around Taunton had changed little in essence over several centuries. It is quite likely that the residents of even nearby settlements would visit Taunton only on market days, their lives being busily occupied with agriculture and other traditional industries.

So what we are seeing in the photographs which follow is a pastoral life which is now no more. Never again would there be such parochial isolation, or such a sharp divide between rural and urban England.

Batts Park 1902 48744

Batts Park Bridge 1906 55804
A reminder of how rural and idyllic the immediate outskirts of Taunton remained until well into the 20th century. Taunton is still a good base for exploring the delightful Somerset countryside.

Bathpool, The Bridge 1902 48745
Bathpool is now very much a suburb of Taunton, with the spread of the Somerset town on one side and the M5 motorway on the other. The Bathpool of a century ago was obviously a much quieter place with life lived at a slower pace. A young girl stands on the bridge - which no longer exists - watching the world go by.

**Bishop's Hull
The Village 1906**
55810
Bishop's Hull has maintained its identity, despite becoming a suburb of Taunton. Much open countryside remains to the west. Buried in the churchyard is William Crotch, a self-taught musical prodigy who became the first principal of the Royal Academy of Music in 1822.

Blagdon Hill, From Taunton 1923 74040
In the rolling countryside now just south of the motorway is the long main street of Blagdon Hill, a popular walking centre for Taunton hikers, who use the extensive network of public footpaths to explore the attractive woodlands and pastures nearby.

Bradford, The Church c1869 4975
Bradford's exquisite little church, seen here at the height of Victoria's reign. Much of the building dates to the Middle Ages, though there is evidence of the earlier Norman building. Not far away are two medieval bridges across the River Tone.

Corfe
The Church of St Nicholas
c1869 4977

Corfe's lovely little church has weathered the attentions of the Victorian restorers much better than many of England's Norman churches. The original Norman font remains in place, and there is some delightful Norman-style carvings on the bench ends and choir stalls.

East Lyng
Main Street c1960 E239010

Not far from the marshes of Athelney, where King Alfred hid from the Danes, are the little settlements of East and West Lyng. Both comprise little more than a main street, part of the ancient highway from Street to Taunton.

◄ **Hatch Beauchamp
The Village c1960** H512001
Hatch Beauchamp
(pronounced Beecham) is
usually referred to by local
people simply as 'Hatch'.
The south chancel window
in the church is dedicated to
John Chard VC, who died in
the village. Chard was the
heroic commanding officer
at the battle of Rorke's Drift
in the Zulu Wars - he was
immortalised in the film
'Zulu', in which he was
played by the actor Stanley
Baker.

Halse, The Village c1955 H498504

A meet of hounds at Halse, a charming old village to the north west of Taunton. In medieval times there was a nunnery and a branch of the Knights Hospitallers at Halse. The present-day village has an historic atmosphere; its little church is particularly fine.

Kingston St Mary The Village c1960

K179006

The broad vale around Kingston, to the north of Taunton, has long been famed for its excellent cider orchards. Samples of the local produce can be bought both on the farms in the vicinity and in the shops of the nearby towns.

Kingston St Mary The Village c1960

K179008

Travellers from Taunton to the Quantock Hills usually go by way of Kingston - and a very picturesque route it is. In the village church is the tomb of John de la Warre, whose family home was at nearby Hestercombe. This doughty warrior helped capture the king of France at the battle of Poitiers in 1356.

Milverton
General View c1955

M371011

Milverton has historic
and legendary links to
powerful figures in the
church. John of
Milverton was created
the English leader of the
Carmelite Friars at a
convention in Paris in
1456. Legend relates
that the old vicarage was
once the country home
of Cardinal Wolsey.

◄ Milverton
A Winding Street
c1955 M371007

As befits its location, well on the way to Exmoor, Milverton was once a thriving centre for the wool trade. Carts and pack ponies would have brought the raw product down from the neighbouring hills, and much of Milverton's street pattern would have evolved at the height of this industry.

▼ North Curry
Church Road c1960
N219013

North Curry is one of several 'Curry villages' which line the higher ground above the marshlands of West Sedgemoor. Some people in the area are still involved in the commercial growing of willow and the manufacture of wickerwork baskets and furniture.

◄ North Curry
River Tone Bridge
c1960 N219015

The Tone is one of several rivers draining these lowlands, and the one that gave Taunton its name. Much of the area was under water when King Alfred used the marshlands as a base for guerrilla operations against the Danes. Today the marshlands are the more peaceful haunt of the fisherman and birdwatcher.

◄ **North Curry
Moor Lane c1960**
N219022
Moor Lane, seen here
with the London House
Stores on the left, leads
to the nearby marshes -
or 'moors' as they are
called in Somerset.
North Curry's
churchyard has a
splendid epitaph for the
lazy: 'My good lads, do
not sit on this stone, on
account you do disfigure
it with your heels. Lean
on if you please. Yours
etc. R. Pocock'.

North Curry
Jubilee Square c1960 N219018
Once a royal manor, North Curry
was granted a weekly market by
King John, who is supposed to
have visited the village on several
occasions. That errant monarch is
credited with the inauguration of
the Reeves Feast, a Boxing Day
distribution of food and coin from
the rich to the poor. This
entertainment survived until
Victorian times, after which it
became a formal charity.

▼ Orchard Portman
The Church 1888

20876
This is really a church
without a village, for only
a few scattered houses
and farms are nearby. A
church has stood here
from at least Norman
times, though most of
the present building is
15th-century, with a
20th-century family
chapel added by Lord
Portman.

◄ Pitminster
**The Church of St Andrew
and St Mary c1869** 4976
To the north of Pitminster is
Poundisford Park, once a
hunting ground for the
Bishops of Winchester. The
park pale (enclosure) can
still be seen by following
the footpaths out of the
village. Sad to say, the old
hunting ground has been
unsympathetically bisected
by the motorway, though a
footbridge carries the
walker across its intrusive
carriageways. The artist
Gainsborough was a regular
visitor to the parish.

**Ruishton
St George's Church and the Vicarage
c1869** 4978
This lovely church with its elaborately-designed tower is one of the joys of Somerset's ecclesiastical architecture. The church remained unfinished at the Reformation, and the more modern additions are not intrusive.

**Stoke St Mary
The Church c1869** 4980
Stoke lies at the foot of the wooded hill of the same name, at the northern edge of the Blackdowns. Stoke St Mary is an ideal centre for exploring this wild and beautiful countryside.

Sherford
The Village 1906 55806
Much of Sherford is now one of Taunton's southern suburbs, though some green areas and the Sherford Stream are still to be found. The latter can be followed for much of its course using some ancient public footpaths.

Sherford 1906 55806x
And what happened to these children of a century ago in the momentous decades of the 20th century? Did they survive two world wars and watch men set foot on the moon?

Sherford 1906 55806V
In the first of two close-up views of the previous scene, we see a group of local children enjoying the delights of the Sherford Stream. Despite the proximity of Taunton, these children would have led a very rural existence, very different to the lifestyles of today's young people.

Trull, The Church of All Saints c1869 4969
One of Somerset's very best churches, All Saints' dates from the 13th century, though it was restored in late Victorian times and during the early 20th century. In the churchyard lie the Victorian children's writer Mrs Juliana Emery and Edward Goldsworthy, the 19th-century chronicler of Taunton.

Trull, Stocks in the Churchyard 1906 55808
Once much feared as a punishment, village stocks are now just a picturesque part of our history. They were mostly used for minor offences such as drunkenness and petty theft. An Act of 1376 decreed that stocks should be set up in every village as a way of controlling unruly labourers.

West Monkton, Coombe c1960 W602011
As the name implies, West Monkton has clerical connections; it was named for the monks of Glastonbury Abbey, which owned the parish. Coombe is a discrete hamlet set in a picturesque valley scarcely a mile from the heart of the village.

West Monkton, The Stocks c1960 W602004
A fine example of a village stocks is to be seen at West Monkton, sheltered beneath the yews of the churchyard. Notice the whipping post on the right. The shelter above is of a later date, for miscreants were seldom protected from the vagaries of the English weather.

West Monkton, The Church of St Augustine c1960 W602003
The yew tree in this churchyard is some 1500 years old, more ancient than the church. A delightful epitaph to a local doctor, William Kinglake, comments: 'Contention's doubtfull, Where two champions bee; Thou hast conquered Death, Now Death hath conquered thee'.

West Monkton, Monkton House c1960 W602002
What is any English village without a 'big house'? Notice the milk bottle on the doorstep.

Westford
The Cloth Mills 1907 58737
Taunton and its surroundings has long been the centre of an
important cloth industry. Indeed, 'Taunton' was a famous type of
serge. Many of the earlier buildings in the towns and villages were
built on the profits of the industry. Old families of Taunton such as
the Weavers, the Clothiers and the Webbs tell of local connections
with this trade.

Index

Frith Book Co Titles

www.francisfrith.co.uk

The Frith Book Company publishes over 100 new titles each year. A selection of those currently available are listed below. For latest catalogue please contact Frith Book Co.

Town Books 96 pages, approx 100 photos. County and Themed Books 128 pages, approx 150 photos (unless specified). All titles hardback laminated case and jacket except those indicated pb (paperback)

Title	ISBN	Price	Title	ISBN	Price
Amersham, Chesham & Rickmansworth (pb)			Derby (pb)	1-85937-367-4	£9.99
	1-85937-340-2	£9.99	Derbyshire (pb)	1-85937-196-5	£9.99
Ancient Monuments & Stone Circles	1-85937-143-4	£17.99	Devon (pb)	1-85937-297-x	£9.99
Aylesbury (pb)	1-85937-227-9	£9.99	Dorset (pb)	1-85937-269-4	£9.99
Bakewell	1-85937-113-2	£12.99	Dorset Churches	1-85937-172-8	£17.99
Barnstaple (pb)	1-85937-300-3	£9.99	Dorset Coast (pb)	1-85937-299-6	£9.99
Bath (pb)	1-85937-419-0	£9.99	Dorset Living Memories	1-85937-210-4	£14.99
Bedford (pb)	1-85937-205-8	£9.99	Down the Severn	1-85937-118-3	£14.99
Berkshire (pb)	1-85937-191-4	£9.99	Down the Thames (pb)	1-85937-278-3	£9.99
Berkshire Churches	1-85937-170-1	£17.99	Down the Trent	1-85937-311-9	£14.99
Blackpool (pb)	1-85937-382-8	£9.99	Dublin (pb)	1-85937-231-7	£9.99
Bognor Regis (pb)	1-85937-431-x	£9.99	East Anglia (pb)	1-85937-265-1	£9.99
Bournemouth	1-85937-067-5	£12.99	East London	1-85937-080-2	£14.99
Bradford (pb)	1-85937-204-x	£9.99	East Sussex	1-85937-130-2	£14.99
Brighton & Hove(pb)	1-85937-192-2	£8.99	Eastbourne	1-85937-061-6	£12.99
Bristol (pb)	1-85937-264-3	£9.99	Edinburgh (pb)	1-85937-193-0	£8.99
British Life A Century Ago (pb)	1-85937-213-9	£9.99	England in the 1880s	1-85937-331-3	£17.99
Buckinghamshire (pb)	1-85937-200-7	£9.99	English Castles (pb)	1-85937-434-4	£9.99
Camberley (pb)	1-85937-222-8	£9.99	English Country Houses	1-85937-161-2	£17.99
Cambridge (pb)	1-85937-422-0	£9.99	Essex (pb)	1-85937-270-8	£9.99
Cambridgeshire (pb)	1-85937-420-4	£9.99	Exeter	1-85937-126-4	£12.99
Canals & Waterways (pb)	1-85937-291-0	£9.99	Exmoor	1-85937-132-9	£14.99
Canterbury Cathedral (pb)	1-85937-179-5	£9.99	Falmouth	1-85937-066-7	£12.99
Cardiff (pb)	1-85937-093-4	£9.99	Folkestone (pb)	1-85937-124-8	£9.99
Carmarthenshire	1-85937-216-3	£14.99	Glasgow (pb)	1-85937-190-6	£9.99
Chelmsford (pb)	1-85937-310-0	£9.99	Gloucestershire	1-85937-102-7	£14.99
Cheltenham (pb)	1-85937-095-0	£9.99	Great Yarmouth (pb)	1-85937-426-3	£9.99
Cheshire (pb)	1-85937-271-6	£9.99	Greater Manchester (pb)	1-85937-266-x	£9.99
Chester	1-85937-090-x	£12.99	Guildford (pb)	1-85937-410-7	£9.99
Chesterfield	1-85937-378-x	£9.99	Hampshire (pb)	1-85937-279-1	£9.99
Chichester (pb)	1-85937-228-7	£9.99	Hampshire Churches (pb)	1-85937-207-4	£9.99
Colchester (pb)	1-85937-188-4	£8.99	Harrogate	1-85937-423-9	£9.99
Cornish Coast	1-85937-163-9	£14.99	Hastings & Bexhill (pb)	1-85937-131-0	£9.99
Cornwall (pb)	1-85937-229-5	£9.99	Heart of Lancashire (pb)	1-85937-197-3	£9.99
Cornwall Living Memories	1-85937-248-1	£14.99	Helston (pb)	1-85937-214-7	£9.99
Cotswolds (pb)	1-85937-230-9	£9.99	Hereford (pb)	1-85937-175-2	£9.99
Cotswolds Living Memories	1-85937-255-4	£14.99	Herefordshire	1-85937-174-4	£14.99
County Durham	1-85937-123-x	£14.99	Hertfordshire (pb)	1-85937-247-3	£9.99
Croydon Living Memories	1-85937-162-0	£9.99	Horsham (pb)	1-85937-432-8	£9.99
Cumbria	1-85937-101-9	£14.99	Humberside	1-85937-215-5	£14.99
Dartmoor	1-85937-145-0	£14.99	Hythe, Romney Marsh & Ashford	1-85937-256-2	£9.99

Available from your local bookshop or from the publisher

Frith Book Co Titles (continued)

Ipswich (pb)	1-85937-424-7	£9.99	St Ives (pb)	1-85937415-8	£9.99
Ireland (pb)	1-85937-181-7	£9.99	Scotland (pb)	1-85937-182-5	£9.99
Isle of Man (pb)	1-85937-268-6	£9.99	Scottish Castles (pb)	1-85937-323-2	£9.99
Isles of Scilly	1-85937-136-1	£14.99	Sevenoaks & Tunbridge	1-85937-057-8	£12.99
Isle of Wight (pb)	1-85937-429-8	£9.99	Sheffield, South Yorks (pb)	1-85937-267-8	£9.99
Isle of Wight Living Memories	1-85937-304-6	£14.99	Shrewsbury (pb)	1-85937-325-9	£9.99
Kent (pb)	1-85937-189-2	£9.99	Shropshire (pb)	1-85937-326-7	£9.99
Kent Living Memories	1-85937-125-6	£14.99	Somerset	1-85937-153-1	£14.99
Lake District (pb)	1-85937-275-9	£9.99	South Devon Coast	1-85937-107-8	£14.99
Lancaster, Morecambe & Heysham (pb)	1-85937-233-3	£9.99	South Devon Living Memories	1-85937-168-x	£14.99
Leeds (pb)	1-85937-202-3	£9.99	South Hams	1-85937-220-1	£14.99
Leicester	1-85937-073-x	£12.99	Southampton (pb)	1-85937-427-1	£9.99
Leicestershire (pb)	1-85937-185-x	£9.99	Southport (pb)	1-85937-425-5	£9.99
Lincolnshire (pb)	1-85937-433-6	£9.99	Staffordshire	1-85937-047-0	£12.99
Liverpool & Merseyside (pb)	1-85937-234-1	£9.99	Stratford upon Avon	1-85937-098-5	£12.99
London (pb)	1-85937-183-3	£9.99	Suffolk (pb)	1-85937-221-x	£9.99
Ludlow (pb)	1-85937-176-0	£9.99	Suffolk Coast	1-85937-259-7	£14.99
Luton (pb)	1-85937-235-x	£9.99	Surrey (pb)	1-85937-240-6	£9.99
Maidstone	1-85937-056-x	£14.99	Sussex (pb)	1-85937-184-1	£9.99
Manchester (pb)	1-85937-198-1	£9.99	Swansea (pb)	1-85937-167-1	£9.99
Middlesex	1-85937-158-2	£14.99	Tees Valley & Cleveland	1-85937-211-2	£14.99
New Forest	1-85937-128-0	£14.99	Thanet (pb)	1-85937-116-7	£9.99
Newark (pb)	1-85937-366-6	£9.99	Tiverton (pb)	1-85937-178-7	£9.99
Newport, Wales (pb)	1-85937-258-9	£9.99	Torbay	1-85937-063-2	£12.99
Newquay (pb)	1-85937-421-2	£9.99	Truro	1-85937-147-7	£12.99
Norfolk (pb)	1-85937-195-7	£9.99	Victorian and Edwardian Cornwall	1-85937-252-x	£14.99
Norfolk Living Memories	1-85937-217-1	£14.99	Victorian & Edwardian Devon	1-85937-253-8	£14.99
Northamptonshire	1-85937-150-7	£14.99	Victorian & Edwardian Kent	1-85937-149-3	£14.99
Northumberland Tyne & Wear (pb)	1-85937-281-3	£9.99	Vic & Ed Maritime Album	1-85937-144-2	£17.99
North Devon Coast	1-85937-146-9	£14.99	Victorian and Edwardian Sussex	1-85937-157-4	£14.99
North Devon Living Memories	1-85937-261-9	£14.99	Victorian & Edwardian Yorkshire	1-85937-154-x	£14.99
North London	1-85937-206-6	£14.99	Victorian Seaside	1-85937-159-0	£17.99
North Wales (pb)	1-85937-298-8	£9.99	Villages of Devon (pb)	1-85937-293-7	£9.99
North Yorkshire (pb)	1-85937-236-8	£9.99	Villages of Kent (pb)	1-85937-294-5	£9.99
Norwich (pb)	1-85937-194-9	£8.99	Villages of Sussex (pb)	1-85937-295-3	£9.99
Nottingham (pb)	1-85937-324-0	£9.99	Warwickshire (pb)	1-85937-203-1	£9.99
Nottinghamshire (pb)	1-85937-187-6	£9.99	Welsh Castles (pb)	1-85937-322-4	£9.99
Oxford (pb)	1-85937-411-5	£9.99	West Midlands (pb)	1-85937-289-9	£9.99
Oxfordshire (pb)	1-85937-430-1	£9.99	West Sussex	1-85937-148-5	£14.99
Peak District (pb)	1-85937-280-5	£9.99	West Yorkshire (pb)	1-85937-201-5	£9.99
Penzance	1-85937-069-1	£12.99	Weymouth (pb)	1-85937-209-0	£9.99
Peterborough (pb)	1-85937-219-8	£9.99	Wiltshire (pb)	1-85937-277-5	£9.99
Piers	1-85937-237-6	£17.99	Wiltshire Churches (pb)	1-85937-171-x	£9.99
Plymouth	1-85937-119-1	£12.99	Wiltshire Living Memories	1-85937-245-7	£14.99
Poole & Sandbanks (pb)	1-85937-251-1	£9.99	Winchester (pb)	1-85937-428-x	£9.99
Preston (pb)	1-85937-212-0	£9.99	Windmills & Watermills	1-85937-242-2	£17.99
Reading (pb)	1-85937-238-4	£9.99	Worcester (pb)	1-85937-165-5	£9.99
Romford (pb)	1-85937-319-4	£9.99	Worcestershire	1-85937-152-3	£14.99
Salisbury (pb)	1-85937-239-2	£9.99	York (pb)	1-85937-199-x	£9.99
Scarborough (pb)	1-85937-379-8	£9.99	Yorkshire (pb)	1-85937-186-8	£9.99
St Albans (pb)	1-85937-341-0	£9.99	Yorkshire Living Memories	1-85937-166-3	£14.99

See Frith books on the internet www.francisfrith.co.uk

FRITH PRODUCTS & SERVICES

Francis Frith would doubtless be pleased to know that the pioneering publishing venture he started in 1860 still continues today. A hundred and forty years later, The Francis Frith Collection continues in the same innovative tradition and is now one of the foremost publishers of vintage photographs in the world. Some of the current activities include:

Interior Decoration

Today Frith's photographs can be seen framed and as giant wall murals in thousands of pubs, restaurants, hotels, banks, retail stores and other public buildings throughout the country. In every case they enhance the unique local atmosphere of the places they depict and provide reminders of gentler days in an increasingly busy and frenetic world.

Product Promotions

Frith products are used by many major companies to promote the sales of their own products or to reinforce their own history and heritage. Frith promotions have been used by Hovis bread, Courage beers, Scots Porage Oats, Colman's mustard, Cadbury's foods, Mellow Birds coffee, Dunhill pipe tobacco, Guinness, and Bulmer's Cider.

Genealogy and Family History

As the interest in family history and roots grows world-wide, more and more people are turning to Frith's photographs of Great Britain for images of the towns, villages and streets where their ancestors lived; and, of course, photographs of the churches and chapels where their ancestors were christened, married and buried are an essential part of every genealogy tree and family album.

Frith Products

All Frith photographs are available Framed or just as Mounted Prints and Posters (size 23 x 16 inches). These may be ordered from the address below. From time to time other products - Address Books, Calendars, Table Mats, etc - are available.

The Internet

Already twenty thousand Frith photographs can be viewed and purchased on the internet through the Frith websites and a myriad of partner sites.

For more detailed information on Frith companies and products, look at these sites:

www.francisfrith.co.uk
www.francisfrith.com
(for North American visitors)

See the complete list of Frith Books at:

www.francisfrith.co.uk

This web site is regularly updated with the latest list of publications from the Frith Book Company. If you wish to buy books relating to another part of the country that your local bookshop does not stock, you may purchase on-line.

For further information, trade, or author enquiries please contact us at the address below:
The Francis Frith Collection, Frith's Barn, Teffont, Salisbury, Wiltshire, England SP3 5QP.
Tel: +44 (0)1722 716 376 Fax: +44 (0)1722 716 881 Email: sales@francisfrith.co.uk

See Frith books on the internet www.francisfrith.co.uk

TO RECEIVE YOUR FREE MOUNTED PRINT

Mounted Print
Overall size 14 x 11 inches

Cut out this Voucher and return it with your remittance for £1.95 to cover postage and handling, to UK addresses. For overseas addresses please include £4.00 post and handling. Choose any photograph included in this book. Your SEPIA print will be A4 in size, and mounted in a cream mount with burgundy rule line, overall size 14 x 11 inches.

Order additional Mounted Prints at HALF PRICE (only £7.49 each*)

If there are further pictures you would like to order, possibly as gifts for friends and family, purchase them at half price (no additional postage and handling required).

Have your Mounted Prints framed*

For an additional £14.95 per print you can have your chosen Mounted Print framed in an elegant polished wood and gilt moulding, overall size 16 x 13 inches (no additional postage and handling required).

---

* IMPORTANT!
These special prices are only available if ordered using the original voucher on this page (no copies permitted) and at the same time as your free Mounted Print, for delivery to the same address

---

Frith Collectors' Guild

From time to time we publish a magazine of news and stories about Frith photographs and further special offers of Frith products. If you would like 12 months FREE membership, please return this form.

Send completed forms to:
The Francis Frith Collection, Frith's Barn, Teffont, Salisbury, Wiltshire SP3 5QP

Voucher for **FREE** and Reduced Price Frith Prints

Picture no.	Page number	Qty	Mounted @ £7.49	Framed + £14.95	Total Cost
		1	**Free of charge***	£	£
			£7.49	£	£
			£7.49	£	£
			£7.49	£	£
			£7.49	£	£
			£7.49	£	£

Please allow 28 days for delivery	*** Post & handling**	**£1.95**
Book Title	**Total Order Cost**	**£**

Please do not photocopy this voucher. Only the original is valid, so please cut it out and return it to us.

I enclose a cheque / postal order for £ . . . . made payable to 'The Francis Frith Collection' OR please debit my Mastercard / Visa / Switch / Amex card *(credit cards please on all overseas orders)*

Number . . . .

Issue No(Switch only) . . . . .Valid from (Amex/Switch) . . . .

Expires . . . . Signature . . . .

Name Mr/Mrs/Ms . . . .

Address . . . .

. . . .

. . . . Postcode . . . .

Daytime Tel No . . . . Valid to 31/12/02

The Francis Frith Collectors' Guild

Please enrol me as a member for 12 months free of charge.

Name Mr/Mrs/Ms . . . .

Address . . . .

. . . .

. . . . Postcode . . . .

Would you like to find out more about Francis Frith?

We have recently recruited some entertaining speakers who are happy to visit local groups, clubs and societies to give an illustrated talk documenting Frith's travels and photographs. If you are a member of such a group and are interested in hosting a presentation, we would love to hear from you.

Our speakers bring with them a small selection of our local town and county books, together with sample prints. They are happy to take orders. A small proportion of the order value is donated to the group who have hosted the presentation. The talks are therefore an excellent way of fundraising for small groups and societies.

Can you help us with information about any of the Frith photographs in this book?

We are gradually compiling an historical record for each of the photographs in the Frith archive. It is always fascinating to find out the names of the people shown in the pictures, as well as insights into the shops, buildings and other features depicted.

If you recognize anyone in the photographs in this book, or if you have information not already included in the author's caption, do let us know. We would love to hear from you, and will try to publish it in future books or articles.

Our production team

Frith books are produced by a small dedicated team at offices in the converted Grade II listed 18th-century barn at Teffont near Salisbury, illustrated above. Most have worked with the Frith Collection for many years. All have in common one quality: they have a passion for the Frith Collection. The team is constantly expanding, but currently includes:

Jason Buck, John Buck, Douglas Burns, Heather Crisp, Isobel Hall, Rob Hames, Hazel Heaton, Peter Horne, James Kinnear, Tina Leary, Hannah Marsh, Eliza Sackett, Terence Sackett, Sandra Sanger, Shelley Tolcher, Susanna Walker, Clive Wathen and Jenny Wathen.

Free Print - see overleaf